Presented to:

~~Wilshire Baptist Church Media Library~~

~~In Honor of~~

~~Mike & Donna Rosamond~~

~~By~~

~~Jeanne Spreier~~

JB
Lov

114460

Best Cowboy in the West

The Story of Nat Love

by Judy Hominick
and Jeanne Spreier

Silver Moon Press
New York

First Silver Moon Press Edition 2001
Copyright © 2001 by Judy Hominick and Jeanne Spreier

The publisher would like to thank Cowboy Mike Searles of Augusta State University
for his historical direction and review. Special thanks also to John and Lois Colburn,
ranchers and farmers in western Kansas.

All rights reserved.
No part of this publication may be reproduced,
except in the case of quotation for articles and reviews,
or stored in any retrieval system, or transmitted in any form
or by any means, electronic, mechanical, photocopying, recording,
or otherwise, without written permission from the publisher.

For information:
Silver Moon Press
New York, NY
(800) 874–3320

Library of Congress Cataloging-in-Publication Data
Hominick, Judy.
  Best cowboy in the West : the story of Nat Love / by Judy Hominick and Jeanne
Spreier.-- 1st Silver Moon Press ed.
    p. cm. -- (Heroes to remember)
  Includes bibliographical references.
  ISBN 1-893110-25-7
  1. Love, Nat, 1854-1921--Juvenile literature. 2. African American cowboys--West
(U.S.)--Biography--Juvenile literature. 3. Cowboys--West (U.S.)--Biography--Juvenile
literature. 4. West (U.S.)--Biography--Juvenile literature. [1. Love, Nat, 1854-1921. 2.
Cowboys. 3. African Americans--Biography.] I. Spreier, Jeanne. II. Title. III. Series.

F594.L892 H66 2001
978'.02'092--dc21
[B]   2001020833

Cover photograph courtesy of **Duke University**, Rare Book, Manuscript, and Special Collections Library,
from the *Life and Adventures of Nat Love better known in the Cattle Country as "Deadwood Dick"—by Himself*:
"The Roping Contest at Deadwood."

Interior photographs courtesy of: the Erwin E. Smith Collection of the Library of Congress at the **Amon Carter
Museum**, Fort Worth Texas: Page 19: LC.S59.017, nitrate negative; Page 21: LC.S611.015, nitrate negative;
Page 26: LC.S59.391, nitrate negative; Page 31: LC.S6.50, nitrate negative; Page 35: LC.S6.180, gelatin sil-
ver print; Page 39: LC.S611.679, nitrate negative; Page 42: LC.S59.351, nitrate negative; Page 43: LC.S6.183,
glass plate negative; Page 49: LC.S6.078, glass plate negative; the **Denver Public Library**, Western History
Collection: Page 33: X21562; **Duke University**, Rare Book, Manuscript, and Special Collections Library,
from the *Life and Adventures of Nat Love better known in the Cattle Country as "Deadwood Dick"—by Himself*:
Pages 55, 57, 58; The **Fort Sill National Historic Landmark**: Page 56; **Idaho State Historical Society**:
Page 29: 78-203.20; **Library of Congress**: Page 2: LC-USZ62-2048; Page 4: LC-B8171-152-A; Page 7: LC-
USF34-044293-D; Page 11: LC-USF34-019873-E; Page 13: LC-USF34-019957-E; Page 16: LC-USF34-
052080-D; Page 47: LC-B8172-1613; Page 48: LC-USZ62-116265; Page 52: LC-USZ62-46841.

To my husband, David,
whose faith in me means everything.

– J.H.

To my love, Scott.

– J.S.

One

Nat quietly tiptoed through the tall grass, hunched close to the ground. The sun was low in the sky and a light evening breeze whispered through the treetops. Nat peered to his left and his right, where he could see his fellow soldiers carefully creeping through the field. The enemy was just a few yards away, in that big oak tree at the edge of the field.

Just a few steps more and then Nat stopped. All the others stopped, too. Nat thrust his hand to the sky and let out a wild war whoop. The ragtag group of boys and girls took their cue from him, raised their own fists in the air and started yelling. They all charged forward to attack the hornet nest in the tree.

With old rags and sticks, the children hit and slapped at the nest, stirring up the hornets. The insects were none too happy to be under attack and flew about stinging the children. Most of the youngsters ran away, some all the way to their log cabins across the field. Nat stayed, determined to beat those hornets. He retreated once, then twice, paying little attention to the stings he received. Always he returned to the nest, beating it again and again with his stick.

At ten years old, Nat was fearless and already he was a leader among slave children on Mr. Love's Tennessee plantation. The Civil War had taken most of the plantation owners and their sons away to fight for the South. Many of the slave men and older boys had escaped to fight with the Union soldiers of the North. Nat wanted to fight the slaveholders, too, but everyone—especially his mother and father—said he was too young. So Nat organized war games with other slave children, trying to imagine what fighting

COME AND JOIN US BROTHERS.
PUBLISHED BY THE SUPERVISORY COMMITTEE FOR RECRUITING COLORED REGIMENTS
1210 CHESTNUT ST. PHILADELPHIA

A recruiting poster in circulation during the Civil War. Many African Americans, both freemen and runaway slaves, joined the Union Army to fight for freedom (Courtesy of the Library of Congress).

for freedom would be like.

The only problem with their games was that no one wanted to pretend to be Rebel soldiers from the South. All the children wanted to be Union soldiers! Nat had thought and thought about whom he might recruit to be a willing enemy. Finally, it occurred to him that the children would have to find an enemy everyone could agree on.

"The hornets' nest," he told his friends. "No one likes hornets."

Everyone decided this was an excellent plan. Hornets were detested by the children and field workers. Here was an enemy worthy of their courage.

Now the battle was nearing an end and only Nat was left to destroy the nest. He had been stung on his bare arms and back and even on his face. But he was determined that not a hornet would be left in this tree.

When Nat finally achieved victory over the hornets, he wearily turned to walk back to the cabin he shared with his parents, his brother, Jordan, and sister, Sally. While he knew he beat the insects, he certainly didn't feel happy. What he felt was pain in almost every part of his body.

"Nat, what a sight you are!" screamed Sally, as he walked through the cabin doorway. "What in the world happened to you?"

"Hornets," Nat said wearily, "I beat the hornets, just like Union soldiers are going to beat the South and set us free."

He flopped on the floor. Sally carefully touched his puffy face. "Are you crazy?"

"Ouch!" Nat wailed. "Don't touch me!"

"Just wait 'til Momma sees you," Sally scolded. "Is she ever going to be mad!"

"Don't you start giving me trouble," Nat moaned to his big sister. "Please, just please get me some wet rags to put on my face."

Sally walked over to the bucket of water and dipped rough-woven rags in the tepid water, wringing them out before bringing them back to Nat. Already Nat felt better as he lay in the dark cabin. The cool, damp cloths eased some of the sting. He knew when his momma got back from her work cooking in the master's house, she would mix a salve to put on his injuries and that, in no time, he would be back to his old, energetic self.

But right now, all Nat could do was lay on the dirt floor of his cabin, with his eyes closed, and enjoy victory in his mind.

Five generations of a South Carolina slave family in 1862, a year into the Civil War. Soon this family, like Nat's, would experience freedom for the first time *(by Timothy H. O'Sullivan, Courtesy of the Library of Congress).*

Two

Freedom is sweet but takes a lot of work, Nat and his family learned. After the Civil War, the family had to decide where to go and what to do. Nat Love and his family were free now, and they could go anywhere and do anything they might like. But it is hard to decide where to go when you haven't been anywhere else in your life.

And as for what to do—Nat's father knew only how to farm, and mostly what he knew how to grow was tobacco and corn.

Some of the freed slaves decided they would work for the Love family just as they did before the war. They stayed on the plantation and worked in the fields in exchange for their cabin, food, and clothes.

"That's not for us," Nat's father said bravely. "If we're free, we're going to live free. We'll make it on our own."

Everyone in the family agreed that was the best

plan. Nat's family rented twenty acres from the Loves. They moved their old cabin to the hill where Nat's father rented the land. They had no money, hardly any food or clothes, and certainly no shoes.

Nat decided what they had was willpower and lots of it. Nat, his brother, and father gathered cane and reeds from the nearby streams and lakes, and at night the three wove chair bottoms by firelight or moonlight. They gathered straw and sticks, and the family made brooms and mats. On Fridays, Nat's father carried all the brooms, mats, and chair bottoms they made that week a dozen miles into the nearest town. There he sold the items, using the few dollars he earned to buy seed to plant.

But that wasn't all. The twenty acres they rented had never had a crop planted on it. The family had to clear land, too, a job that was difficult when it was hot and sunny and miserable when it was rainy. "Get up, boys," Nat's father called each morning, as the sun rose. "Work won't wait for you."

By the time they were done in the fields every day, they were too exhausted to care that supper would be the same thing they had had for breakfast that morning—and for supper the night before.

Nat's mother cooked bread made with bran, cracklings, and a little salt, all mixed with buttermilk. She wrapped the dough in a cabbage leaf and covered it with hot coals. The family called it ash cake.

After eating, Nat and Jordan headed out to the fields to pull up more weeds and bushes.

"It would have been easier to get land that had

A sharecropper chopping firewood from slabs, Green County, Georgia. This photograph was taken in 1941, but life hadn't changed much for poor farmers since the 1860s. Families had to work together to survive *(by Jack Delano, Courtesy of the Library of Congress)*.

already been farmed," Jordan grumbled one day.

"Easier wouldn't be better," Nat said. "Easier would mean we'd pay more for the land. We don't have anything as it is now. Poor Momma's used to cooking with fine meats and butter and all sorts of fancy things, like sugar and eggs. All she's got now is plain old cracklings."

"Remember when you used to sneak into the garden at the master's house to pick turnips and potatoes, Nat? That's what we need now! A turnip would taste so good right now."

Being the youngest, Nat sometimes had been overlooked when he was a tot on the plantation. With his momma in the big house, and Sally helping, too, and his father and big brother in the fields, Nat was often forgotten in the bustle of work. He learned when he was just a tyke that tasty vegetables were growing near the kitchen. When he got hungry, all he had to do was pick them.

"I sure got in trouble when I got caught," Nat said, laughing at the memory. "But I sure got good at crawling through that garden and not being seen. I knew just which trees to hide behind and just which rows were easiest to reach. And remember how Momma would laugh when I pulled corn out of my shirt, or peas or peppers? She never said I did right, but she sure didn't mind having those good things to eat.

"That's what I'm thinking about," Nat said. "How good this corn is going to taste once it's ready to pick."

"I can taste it already," Jordan said.

The boys worked on; every week their father came home with another sack full of seeds. Into the rich, dark earth they carefully dropped the seeds, one at a time, making sure none went to waste. Tall, green leafy stalks of corn, bushy tobacco plants, and other vegetables soon grew on the hillside.

The family looked proudly at their little patch of crops and knew that, for the first time in their lives, all their hard work produced something they had never had before: a future.

Three

Nat plopped down on the dirt next to Jordan. The brothers sat quietly, looking at the broad tobacco leaves in front of them—and the row of plants ahead of them. From the plants came a faint click-clicking noise.

"I hate this," Nat finally said to his brother.

Jordan, sitting with his hands in his lap, said nothing.

"If Daddy finds out we're not pulling off those worms, he'll thrash us," Nat said.

Jordan gingerly lifted the tip of a tobacco leaf. Underneath was a rotund green worm, about the length of the boys' largest finger, with an ugly horn poking from its head. It slowly munched the precious tobacco leaf. The boys could hear the faint click-click as its jaws crunched the leaf.

"You get this one. I'll get the next," Jordan said bravely.

"I have a better idea," Nat said. "Let's use a stick to knock the worm off the leaf. Then we can smash it with a rock."

"We're going to tear the leaves, Nat. Then Daddy will thrash us anyway," Jordan said.

"OK, since you're so brave, Jordan, you pick off the worms and I'll smash them." No way did Nat want to touch those worms. The worms wrapped around your fingers and started nibbling on them. It was plain disgusting.

"Hold that leaf up," Nat ordered, reaching for a stick. He swiped at the fat worm. The worm stayed planted on the leaf and kept munching. Nat hit it harder. Nothing happened.

"Nat, you better be careful," Jordan warned.

Nat looked at the worm's beady eyes, its stubby legs, its huge mouth. He gave it a good thwack. The worm dropped to the dirt and started crawling away. Nat brought down a rock and felt a satisfying scrunch as he smashed the worm. He was victorious!

"Oh, Nat!" Jordan wailed. "Look at the leaf. It's torn. It won't be worth nearly as much now. We better not let Daddy see this."

Nat quickly picked the shredded leaf and ran to the nearby woods. He hid it under a pile of sticks. When he came back, Jordan looked aghast.

"Nat, you can't do that! We won't have any tobacco to sell if we rip off those leaves," Jordan said.

"Do *you* want to pick the worms?" Nat asked. He already knew the answer. No!

Nat lifted a leaf and scraped off another worm.

No damage this time, but the next three leaves, lower leaves and hard to see, all got ripped. Nat left those on the plants. It went that way all day. Although some leaves escaped damage, Nat tore many with the stick. The ones that were easy to see Nat picked and hid in the woods.

Late that night, after their father came in from the fields, he called the boys to him.

"I found a pile of torn tobacco leaves in the woods," he started. Both boys stared at him. They knew what was coming next.

A sharecropper's son goes up and down the long rows worming tobacco, Wake County, North Carolina, 1939 *(by Dorothea Lange, Courtesy of the Library of Congress)*.

The following day, despite the tobacco horn-worms' disgusting appearance, the boys carefully picked them off the tobacco leaves and dropped them in a bucket.

That first year's tobacco crop paid rent on the farm. The leftover corn and vegetables the family had to make last through the cold winter for food.

Through the dark winter days, with chill seeping into their cabin and snow burying the woodpile, Sally, Jordan, and Nat stayed busy. Even though they were free, no school would accept former slaves as students. Their father, who had learned to read a little, prodded them to study the A-B-Cs.

"Daddy, this doesn't make any sense," Jordan whined one day.

"Making sense isn't important," his father responded. "Learning it is. Just keep at it. Soon enough you'll know more than me." He sat next to Jordan, determined his son would stick to his reading lesson.

In that one winter, the three children didn't learn much. But it was more than they were allowed to learn during all the days of slavery.

In spring, the family started their second year of freedom with great joy. The children's father worked a few weeks for a nearby plantation owner. As payment, the Loves borrowed the owner's horses and plows for their own planting. The family eagerly tilled the moist earth, carefully burying seeds and hoping this year's larger crop would mean a little extra money at the end of the summer. Everyone weeded the rows of corn, squashed tobacco hornworms, and took joy in the young green shoots coming from the ground.

Then tragedy struck.

One day, Nat's father couldn't get out of bed. "Daddy," Jordan said, "you just get better. Nat and I will take care of the farm today."

"You're good boys," his father replied weakly. "You take care of the crops, and I'll just sleep awhile. I'm just bone tired, that's all."

But the next day, their father felt the same. And the day after that.

Plowing corn with a mule and plow, Person County, North Carolina, 1939. For poor farmers in the 1800s and early 1900s, plowing took muscle, determination, and lots of time *(by Dorothea Lange, Courtesy of the Library of Congress).*

"What if Papa doesn't get up soon?" Jordan asked Nat when they started hoeing for the fourth day without their father nearby. "Then what?"

"We'll just have to do as we promised," Nat said seriously. "We'll take care of the farm."

The next day, the boys got up before dawn to get ready for another day of work. Their mother was already up, sitting quietly next to her husband's still body. Tears ran down her cheeks.

"Your father died last night," she said simply.

Nat looked at his mother and brother with a determined face. "There's no use weeping," he said grimly. "We have work to do. We have a crop to get in. We must get ready for winter. There's no one to help us but each other."

Four

Nat had to do something—and quickly. No one in his family had shoes, their only clothes were old and tattered, and most days they were hungry. The harvest had been good but not great. The year that started with much promise was turning grim. They worked hard all week. Some days Nat worked in the fields, planting crops, weeding, even picking those horrible tobacco hornworms. Some days, he and his mother went into the woods to pick blackberries. They sold these in town for a few cents a bucket. Other days, he gathered walnuts, hickory nuts, or chestnuts in the nearby woods, throwing them into a little wooden sled he made. These he sold in town, too. Always he spent the money on seed and a few things for cooking, like salt or flour.

Some days, fourteen-year-old Nat just wanted to cry. One day, after wild pigs ate their entire day's worth of berry picking, his mother did cry. "There are plenty more where those came from," Nat said to his mother, trying to console her.

"My boy, whatever happens to you, you never get discouraged," his mother responded. Nat worked into the night to refill the baskets.

No matter how much there was to do, Sunday was always a day of rest. For Nat, it meant a day of play—of running through the woods, playing hide-and-seek or tag.

One Sunday was different, though. "Momma," Nat called out. "I'll be back by sundown."

A sharecropper and his wife stripping and grading tobacco, near Carr, North Carolina, 1939 *(by Marion Post Walcott, Courtesy of the Library of Congress)*.

"Stay out of trouble, boy," his mother responded. "You know we all depend on you." Nat barely heard his mother's warning before he was outside. He knew just what he was going to do.

The lush grass sparkled with morning dew. It felt good on Nat's bare feet. He cut through the woods, heading down the hill to the road that led to town. When Nat got to the road, he headed away from town. Mr. Williams owned a horse ranch farther up the road. He had two boys about Nat's age. Nat and the elder boy had made a plan. If Nat came out Sunday morning when the rest of the family was at church, the son would pay Nat ten cents for every wild colt he managed to ride long enough so that the colt would settle down and not buck.

Ten cents looked like a lot of money to Nat.

Nat had ridden calm ponies, but the Williams' untamed horses presented a challenge. Even so, ten whole cents was worth the risk.

"Nat, I was afraid you wouldn't show," the boy called from the corral as Nat walked up.

"I had to do chores before I left," Nat responded. He looked at the brown colt pacing the corral, its wild black mane flowing in the breeze.

"Here he is," the boy said. "I don't want you to use a bridle, in case my father comes home early from church. You need to be able to slip off his back and pretend we're just talking if he shows up."

Nat had never broken a horse before. And now he'd have to do it by staying astride using only his legs for balance and his hands to grasp the mane!

"How am I going to get up on him?" Nat asked. The horse hadn't stopped moving since Nat arrived.

"We'll get him into that stall over there, and then you just jump aboard," the boy said with far more confidence than Nat felt.

Nat kicked at the dirt with his toes. This was going to be the hardest ten cents he'd ever earned.

"OK," Nat answered, slowly climbing over the fence of the corral. He and the boy waved their arms, scaring the horse back into the barn. The colt swung his head back and forth, looking at the two boys. Slowly he backed into a stall, prancing with each step. The boys slammed the half-door of the stall shut as soon as the colt was in.

Nat climbed on top of the door. He waited silently for the horse to come near. *My momma would cry if she saw me*, Nat thought. The colt circled the stall several times, never slowing enough for Nat to jump onto his back.

"Hurry on up, Nat," the boy called. "We ain't got all day. My daddy's going to be home soon."

"Hush," Nat said, sitting stock still. The colt came over to sniff him. *It's now or never*, Nat thought.

Quick as a flash, he swung a leg over the young horse's back, grabbed his mane, and stared straight ahead. "Open the door!" he yelled.

The boy swung the stall door open. Nat gripped the horse with his legs till his knees hurt. He buried his hands in the mane, his fingernails digging into his palms. The horse charged into the corral and spun on his rear hooves, almost throwing Nat to the ground. Dust and dirt flew everywhere as the horse charged around the corral. Nat squeezed his eyes shut to keep the dirt out.

Nat couldn't see where he was going. But he could hear the joy in the Williams boy's voice, as he yelled from the fence. "Yeehaw! You're doing it Nat, you're doing it!"

A cowboy, Montclavio Lucero, on a rearing bronco in the LS Corral, LS Ranch, Texas, 1907. Nat began breaking horses when he was only thirteen or fourteen. Unlike the cowboy in this photograph, Nat rode broncos bareback without the help of saddle or reins *(by Erwin E. Smith, Courtesy of the Amon Carter Museum)*.

Five

Slowly life at the Love's small cabin improved. Chestnuts earned Nat a dollar a bushel; walnuts and hickory nuts each earned him fifty cents a bushel. After one successful trip to town with nuts and produce to sell, Nat even stopped at the general store to buy his mother a brilliant red dress.

All this time, Nat knew he didn't want to stay at the small farm planting crops. He'd heard stories about life out west, about cowboys and buffalo and cattle drives. With each horse he broke for the Williams family, his skills with horses improved.

Farm life was the same year in and year out— planting, hoeing, harvesting. Nat never traveled farther than a few miles from his family cabin. But he heard that there were fortunes to be made in the West. Nat wanted adventure; he wanted to meet new people; he wanted to try something else. He yearned to explore the world! Nat decided he must leave home.

One day, Nat mentioned his dream to his mother. "Son, you have no clothes and no money. How long would you last away from home?" his mother said. "It's a silly idea. You'll just make yourself sick worrying about it."

Nat said nothing. But he knew, some day, he would head west.

A few months later, Nat was in town selling produce when he saw a crowd had gathered in front of a store. There, a man named Johnson was raffling off a beautiful horse for fifty cents a chance. Nat listened to the coins jangling in his pocket. Raffles weren't the way to get rich, Nat knew. Mr. Johnson saw him hesitate.

A group of African American cowboys posed in connection with a fair in Bonham, Texas, 1911. Nat's dream of becoming a cowboy was one that was shared by many other African American men and boys. The cowboy profession in the Old West was one of the most equal opportunity careers of the time. Worth and respect were, for the most part, determined by performance rather than skin color *(by Erwin E. Smith, Courtesy of the Amon Carter Museum)*.

"Come on boy, you'd like this fine horse, wouldn't you?" the man prodded.

Nat said nothing.

"Just fifty cents a chance. Surely this horse is worth fifty cents!" the man laughed. Another man stepped forward to buy a chance.

Nat reached into his pocket and felt the cool coins. *That's a bushel of walnuts*, Nat thought. *Winning that horse is easily worth a bushel of walnuts.* Nat knew his momma would be angry if she found he had wasted money on a raffle.

Nat stepped forward with five dimes. "Ha, ha!" Mr. Johnson called out. "I knew you were a smart boy." He pocketed Nat's money and gave him a slip of paper with a number on it. Nat felt sick to his stomach. He had probably just wasted his fifty cents.

The horse pranced before the crowd of men. Others stepped up with their coins, each getting a slip of paper in return. Nat patted the horse's smooth flanks, then walked forward to let its soft nostrils nuzzle his hand. *This horse*, Nat thought, *could be my way west.*

"All right," Mr. Johnson yelled. "Last chance for this fine horse! Ladies and gentlemen, this horse will go to the lucky winner in two minutes."

Several more people stepped forward to buy a raffle ticket. Nat's heart sank. With so many people buying chances, he would never win the raffle.

"We're ready to draw the winner," Mr. Johnson said in a loud voice. He selected a girl from the crowd to pick a slip of paper from his hat. "Number 115.

Who has number 115?"

Several men dropped their papers to the ground and turned to leave. Nat stared at his paper in disbelief. There it was—right in front of him. Number 115. "I do, I do," Nat yelled, holding up his winning ticket.

Mr. Johnson laughed. "So you do. But what in the world are you going to do with this fine horse? Do you have a saddle or bridle? Do you even have a place to keep him?"

Nat hung his head. He didn't even have a change of clothes, much less a saddle. "Tell you what I'm going to do," Mr. Johnson said. "I'll buy that horse from you for fifty dollars." Nat looked at Mr. Johnson. "You want to sell that horse for fifty dollars?" he asked. Mr. Johnson had sold almost two hundred chances. He would still pocket almost fifty dollars, even if he bought the horse from Nat. The crowd laughed as they heard the offer.

"I sure do," Nat responded. He accepted fifty one-dollar bills from Mr. Johnson.

Nat turned on his heel and headed home, with growing dreams of heading west.

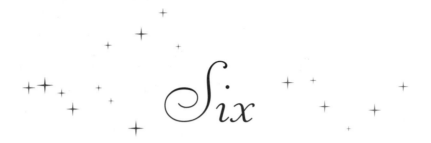

Six

"No way are you leaving this house, Nat Love," his mother wailed when he walked in the cabin door with fifty dollars and grand plans. "This is your home. You need to stay."

"But Momma, this is my chance," the young boy said. "I'll split the money with you. But please understand, Momma, if I don't go now, I'll never get to see the world."

Nat's mother turned away. She wouldn't talk about Nat going west. Nat tucked the money in a sack he kept hidden in the cabin floor. He'd use that money to go west, he knew.

Harvest was good in 1868. The family sold their crop and had money left to save for the winter. Nat's uncle moved in with them to help with the farm. "Now, Momma, now's when I need to go," Nat said.

Nat took a few dollar bills from his sack and went

to town to buy underwear—which he'd never had—and a few other things for his trip. He put his few belongings in a satchel, hid the remaining money in a purse hanging around his neck, and kissed his family goodbye.

Nat Love left his Tennessee cabin and headed west in February 1869. He was fifteen years old.

Sometimes Nat got rides from farmers as he headed west, but mostly he walked along the dirt roads, sleeping under the stars and eating what little food he could scavenge. He knew he wanted to be in Kansas. That's where cattle were driven so they could be loaded onto trains and shipped east. Where there were cattle there were cowboys. And Nat had heard grand stories about cowboys who rode prancing horses and lived wild, exciting lives. Cowboys possessed all the freedom of the wide plains. After so many long years as a plantation slave and a poverty-stricken farmer, a chance to make it on his own in the Wild West was exactly what Nat wanted.

Finally he made it to Dodge City, a scruffy town high on the prairie in Kansas. Cattle ranches all over the Southwest drove their herds to Dodge City. The cattle were sold to companies that shipped them in railroad cars to huge meat packing plants in Kansas City or Chicago.

After spending months on the dusty trails, cowboys got wild in Dodge City. Saloons and dance halls lined the streets. Nat walked through town, hoping to find an outfit that would hire him. Plenty of the cowboys were former slaves, just like him. And no matter what their race, the cowboys sat together, talking, eating, arguing. They walked together, stopping in stores to buy things they needed on the trail. But none of them had time to talk to Nat.

Early one morning, Nat headed to the outskirts of town, where the cowboys gathered around campfires, eating breakfast after sleeping under the stars with their outfits. "Hey, kid, come on over and get some chuck," one of the men called.

A stern-looking man standing at the back of an open wagon ladled a steaming mixture of beans and meat onto a plate, added a biscuit, and handed it to Nat without a word. "Don't mind Cookie," said one of the cowboys. "He lost a bundle at the saloon playing poker yesterday and isn't feeling too perky this morning."

Spur Ranch, Texas. Some Spur cowboys resting and working around the chuck and hoodlum wagons, 1910. The chuck wagon, where food was prepared, was the center of cowboy life on the trail. The hoodlum wagon carried bedrolls, firewood, and other essentials *(by Erwin E. Smith, Courtesy of the Amon Carter Museum)*.

The men all laughed, and Nat eagerly dug into the first warm meal he'd had in two months. "So, boss, we didn't lose many cattle on this trip, did we?" said the gruff cowboy next to Nat.

"Nope," the boss answered. "They'll be pleased back at the ranch. When we loaded 'em up on the train, we counted 1,973 head of cattle. We hit the trail with two thousand."

"I bet we lost about ten head when those cattle rustlers hit us in Oklahoma Territory," said another cowboy. "Dressed to look like Indians. Can you believe? They didn't fool me though."

Nat chewed his food slowly, not wanting to miss a bit of exciting news about the trail drive.

"But we didn't lose a single man," the boss said, slurping from his tin coffee cup. "That's rough, when you lose a cowboy to an attack, rough when you lose a man to a rattlesnake bite, too."

After breakfast, Nat went up to the boss. "I'd like a job with your outfit," he said.

"Aw, a young boy like you! Cattle thieves and rattlesnakes don't scare you? You haven't heard the worst—about stampedes that go on for thirty miles or more and hail the size of apples hammering your head and Indian attacks," the boss said.

"Sounds just fine to me," Nat said.

"Can you ride a wild horse?" the boss asked.

Nat's heart jumped. "Yes, sir," he fairly sang. All those Sundays at the Williams farm would pay off.

"If you can, you've got a job," the boss said. "Bronco Jim, go saddle up ol' Good Eye. Let's see

what this kid's got in him." At the mention of Good
Eye, the cowboys all laughed again.

Nat followed Bronco Jim, also a former slave, out
to the corral. "You pay attention to this horse,"
Bronco Jim said. "He's a pitcher."

"I'm a good rider," Nat assured Bronco Jim.

"You may be fine, but you've never ridden Good
Eye. Keep steady and don't give up."

By the time Good Eye was saddled, cowboys circled the corral, their breath steamy in the cool
morning air. None of them expected Nat to stay on
the bucking horse. Nat carefully climbed into the
saddle, thinking this would be a whole lot easier
than riding bareback as he had in Tennessee.

Bronco Jim let go of the horse, and Nat snapped
to attention. The horse spun away from the fence,
turning on its back hooves. Nat sat tight in the saddle. Good Eye raced across the corral, turning at the
last second away from the fence. Nat squeezed his
knees as the horse rocked forward on his front
hooves, kicking his back legs in the air.

The cowboys started whooping, waving their
slouch hats in the air. Good Eye quit bucking and
loped around the corral. Nat stayed alert for any sign
that the horse would kick up his hooves again.

"Hey boss, he's sure as shooting taking the kinks
out of Good Eye," Nat heard one cowboy yell.

"I guess he's done a good job for such a boy," the
boss yelled back. "Hey you," he called to Nat. "Get
off that horse and come talk to me."

When Good Eye slowed to a trot and started

walking around the corral, Nat slipped out of the saddle and headed for the boss, who was still leaning across the fence. "I thought you was a tenderfoot for sure," the boss said. "But we have room for a fellow like you. This is the Duval outfit; we're from west Texas. How about thirty dollars a month?"

Nat's eyes grew wide. That was more money than he was ever likely to see at one time back in Tennessee. "The Duval outfit?" Nat said. "Sure. Sure I'd like to ride with you."

"You got any gear?" The boss asked. "I guess not. We'll get you in town and get you set up. You'll need a saddle, a bridle, a couple of blankets, chaps, spurs, and a Colt 45. You got a name?"

"Nat Love," the teen said.

Tracy Thompson, an Idaho bucking-horse champion, Idaho, 1900 *(Courtesy of the Idaho State Historical Society)*.

Seven

"Toss that bedroll up here," Cookie yelled at Nat. Cookie stood in the chuck wagon catching the blankets cowboys had rolled and tied with a leather strap after they got up that chilly morning. Steam from the horses' muzzles mixed with the cowboys' breath and white wisps of steam rising from coffee mugs. The cowboys hoisted their saddles, which just an hour ago had served as bed pillows, onto the backs of their mounts. Buckles jangled and cowboys joked as they got ready to head south to the Duval ranch in the Texas panhandle.

"This is going to be an easy trip," the boss assured Nat, once all the men were up in their saddles and on the trail. "No cattle to slow us down. We might make forty miles a day—maybe more."

"*Hola, amigo,*" the boss yelled to one of the cowboys walking past.

"What did you say, Boss?" Nat asked. Nat had

discovered that no one was called by his real name. The trail boss was Boss, the cook, Cookie. All the cowboys had a nickname, like Bronco Jim or Wild Bob. For some reason that Nat couldn't explain, Boss had begun calling him Red River Dick.

The boss looked at him and smiled. "*Hola, amigo.* Hello, friend. Didn't you know those cowboys over there don't speak much English? They're from Mexico. Great cowboys—*vaqueros.* You have a lot to learn, Red River Dick, if you want to work with a Texas outfit. You better start learning Spanish. *Adiós.*"

The boss dug his spurs into his horse's sides and moved quickly toward the cowboys he had been calling. Nat looked at Bronco Jim, riding nearby.

"Bronco Jim, is the boss fooling me?" Nat asked.

J. A. Ranch, Texas, around a campfire having a late dinner, 1907. Cowboys worked long hours, sometimes eating dinner and breakfast in the dark so they could spend every hour of daylight on the trail *(by Erwin E. Smith, Courtesy of the Amon Carter Museum).*

"Will I get kicked out of the outfit because I don't speak Spanish?"

"Nope," the old cowboy said. "You'll learn Spanish soon enough though. Every day, learn one word. Before you know it, you'll be talking like you were born down in Old Mexico."

"So teach me a word for today—one of the words Boss used," Nat begged.

"*Sí, amigo*," Bronco Jim responded.

" 'See?' I know that word," Nat said, confused.

"*Sí* means yes. *Amigo* means friend. There, you know two words now."

When the cowboys stopped for their noontime meal, Nat walked up to one of the *vaqueros*.

"*Amigo*," he said, sticking out his hand.

All the cowboys laughed at the fifteen-year-old's earnest attempt to learn a new language.

"Yes, Red River Dick," the cowboy answered in English. "You are a friend, too."

*   *   *

"How you doing?" the trail boss asked Nat as they stopped the first night, twelve hours after leaving Dodge City. They had just passed the cutoff to Ashland, Kansas. The little road headed west from the Dodge City Trail, a well-worn route the Duval outfit was taking back to Texas.

"I never knew my hind parts could hurt so much," Nat said, after sliding off his horse. He tried not to limp.

The fellows chuckled as they watched Nat

gingerly step toward Cookie's campfire. Nat untied the bandanna around his neck and wiped the grime from his face. He tucked it into one of the deep pockets of his new vest. His clothes, which had looked so shiny and new just yesterday, already showed wear. From his flannel shirt to the plain leather chaps, which strapped around his brown wool trousers to protect them from getting snagged on brush, everything was covered with trail dust.

He knew there were buckles somewhere to undo the chaps and free him from the heavy leather. "Ooh," Nat groaned as he reached down. All the cowboys laughed again. "If you think you're sore now, just wait 'til tomorrow morning," Cookie called from the fire. "Nothing a cup of coffee won't fix, though. Grub's on!"

A group of Oklahoma law enforcement officers on horseback between 1880–1910. *left to right* Amos Maytubby, Zeke Miller, Neely Factor, and Bob L. Fortune *(Courtesy of the Denver Public Library).*

$\mathcal{E}ight$

our years could have been a lifetime for Nat. No one from Tennessee would have recognized this rough-and-tumble cowboy who could land his lariat over the horns of a bull as easily as he might toss his blanket on a bunk. By 1872, Nat had hired on at the Pete Gallinger ranch in Arizona Territory, where he rode across thousands of acres, rounding up cows and their calves at branding time and steer when an order came to sell to meat packers in the east or ranchers up north.

One night the boss came into the cowboys' low, log bunkhouse. "We got an order to get a herd down in Old Mexico and drive it to the Powder River," he announced to the cowboys. Some of them played cards in the dim firelight.

"Powder River in Wyoming Territory?" Nat asked.

"Yup. We'll be going down south to pick up five hundred head of four-year-old longhorns," Boss said. "Then we'll move north through Texas, Oklahoma, Kansas, and Nebraska. We'll go on to the Shoshone Mountains where the Mitchell spread is. Shouldn't be too much of a problem. Those four-year-olds are easy to move."

The cowboys put away their cards. Once the order for cattle came, work started immediately. They'd be leaving the next morning for a round up south of the border. They wouldn't be back to the ranch for four months or more.

More than a month later, the cowboys waded through prairie bluegrass tall enough to hide a man. It waved in the gentle breeze. The Gallinger outfit was on high alert as it herded steer through Oklahoma's Indian Territory.

"Look, over there," one of the cowboys yelled, pointing to grass that moved in an unnatural way.

Mat Walker, wagon boss for the Matador, rounding up cattle on Doodlebug, famous Matador cutting horse, Matador Ranch, Texas, 1908 *(by Erwin E. Smith, Courtesy of the Amon Carter Museum)*.

"Might be a deer," the boss said. "Don't get easy on the trigger."

As the boss said that, two grim looking men stepped in front of him, their guns drawn. The boss stopped. The cattle and cowboys, lined up behind them for almost a mile, bunched up behind him as they stopped.

"Looks like you boys mean to say hello," the boss said easily.

The two men laughed. "Hello, and looks like a fine herd of steer you got there," one of the men said. "Guess you wouldn't miss ten of those cattle as payment to us to guarantee you make it through to Kansas all right."

"No way!" the boss roared back. "This is a public trail we're taking north. We don't owe you a thing." Cowboys who had been at the rear of the herd rode forward to see what was happening. They pulled their pistols as they neared the front.

"It's all right, boys," the boss yelled back at them. "Put your guns away. These men are just saying hello."

Seeing the number of armed cowboys, the two men moved back into the grass. The boss turned in his saddle where his men, cattle, and horses stood like statues, unmoving. "Boys, we have cattle to move!" He waved his hat above his head, heading north on the trail, the point riders and steer falling in behind him, the drag riders waiting to make sure no cattle were left behind.

"Don't think those cattle rustlers have left us

alone," Boss said that evening, as the cowboys ate dinner. "Those men weren't about to offer protection. They just were out and out trying to steal our cattle. Keep your boots on, men, and your guns handy tonight."

That evening, half the cowboys lay on the prickly grass and fell sound asleep. Near midnight, the cowboys on watch gave the danger call. They'd seen rustlers near the herd, trying to start a stampede.

"Quick," the boss yelled to two cowboys, already mounted on their horses. "Get in front and don't let the herd string out on us. If it starts stampeding north, we'll never find them all. The rest of you boys get over to each side and keep turning the cattle back and forth through the grass. It's so blasted dark I don't think those rustlers will be able to see us long enough to get in a good shot."

Nat galloped over to the western edge of their campground and rode through the grass, hoping his horse wouldn't step in a snake hole or trip on a boulder in the dark. As the longhorns got closer, he shouted, scaring them so they reversed their direction.

Six hours later, dawn broke gray across the grasslands. "I'm beat. I can't keep this up much longer," Nat called to another cowboy, who was shading his eyes as he looked off to the east.

"Hey, Red River, look over there," the cowboy called back, pointing to four men galloping across the prairie, silhouetted against the sunrise. "There go our troubles. Guess we'll finally be able to get some rest."

Nine

"Hey, Red River," a cowboy called out to Nat. They were riding the range, rounding up three-year-old longhorns for a drive to Dakota Territory. "This brand looks funny to me." He pointed to the mark cowboys burned into the hide of the longhorn's flank with a hot iron. The brand was used on the open range to identify which ranch owned the animal. Each ranch had a different brand. This brand, Nat knew right away, didn't belong to any ranch he knew—and he knew all the ranches from Texas to Arizona and north to Kansas. The brand didn't look exactly like the Gallinger brand but close.

"That brand's sure as shooting been fixed," Nat determined. "Those rustlers are getting better all the time, though." He pointed out how an extra bar had been burned into the steer's hide, changing the look of the Gallinger symbol. "This one's ours for

Branding scene, 1910. Branding is a necessary part of the cattle industry. Symbols are burned into the cow's flesh so that cowboys can tell which cattle belong to each ranch. Nat's job as a brand reader was essential to running the ranch *(by Erwin E. Smith, Courtesy of the Amon Carter Museum).*

certain," he said. "Hey," Nat yelled at the steer, moving him over with others. "I guess we better head back to the ranch," he said.

Now a cowboy for seven years, Nat was a leader of his outfit and eager to hit the trail again. Even though this year, 1876, people across the United States were celebrating the nation's centennial, cowboys across the West couldn't take a break.

For the next three or four months, Nat knew, the days would be filled with snake bites, thunderstorms, stampedes, and the same old food—beans, biscuits, and beef jerky.

Back at the ranch, the bunkhouse buzzed with work. Cowboys cleaned their guns and rifles, oiled their boots, and made sure their saddle stitching was strong. Nat walked in and threw his gear down. He turned around and grabbed some empty bottles as he left. A few hundred yards behind the bunkhouse was a ravine. Nat walked down there with the bottles, his Colt 45, and his pockets stuffed with bullets.

A large wooden plank rested across two boulders in the draw. Broken glass littered the ground underneath it. Just last week, ranch hands held a shooting competition. Nat beat everyone in the outfit—but he still wanted to practice.

He set the bottles up along the board and then stepped back 150 feet. The bottles glistened in the Arizona sun. Nat cocked his new Colt revolver.

Ping. Glass tinkled as it fell to the ground. Nat shot again. Ping. Two for two. He aimed for the third and fourth bottle. With six shots, he shattered all six bottles. He walked to the board to set up the biggest pieces of the broken bottles for more target practice.

"Hey, Red River, boss is looking for you," yelled a cowboy, walking down the ravine toward him. "I said, 'If I know Red, he's out shootin' rattlesnakes again.' He sent me to fetch you."

"Let me get off these last six shots," Nat replied, as he paced away from the targets, reloading his Colt 45 as he walked. He spun quickly on his heels to face the broken bottles.

Ping, ping, ping, ping, ping, ping.

Six more times, he heard glass splinters falling to the ground. "Whooee," the other man said in admiration. "Maybe it pays to spend your time shooting rattlers."

Ten

Cowboys gulped their last cup of coffee on the ranch in the morning darkness before they hurried to the remuda, the herd of horses that would travel with them all the way to Dakota Territory. The cowboys needed fresh horses, sometimes three times a day, during the months-long journey to deliver the herd. A Dakota rancher planned to fatten these cattle up before selling them to meat companies. Two wranglers had eighty horses picked out for the cowboys. Nat, with his saddle, bridle, and horse blanket slung over an arm, looked around for his favorite mount and clucked the gelding over to his side. Nat quickly saddled up and rode back to the bunkhouse to get the last of his gear.

Throwing a hitch around a post with the reins, he went inside the dark bunkhouse one last time. His Winchester rifle was in its leather case, under his bunk. Nat grabbed the gun, his bedroll, and slicker.

Even if the day started clear, no telling when rain would hit. Back outside, Nat slid the rifle into a special loop on the side of his saddle and tied the slicker behind his saddle.

Cowboys busily strapped on their spurs and chaps, checking their saddles one last time, and tossing bedrolls in the hoodlum wagon. The cattle were quiet. Vapor from their breath rose in the cool March air, making the pasture look misty. Cowboys who had stood guard for the last watch finished a quick breakfast and stopped by the remuda to get fresh horses.

"All right, boys," the boss yelled out in the predawn light. "Let's get a move on."

The boss spurred his horse to the front of the

Cowboy Emory Sager catching mounts from the remuda held by a rope corral, Shoe Bar Ranch, Texas, 1912. The remuda of horses traveled with the cowboys on long journeys *(by Erwin E. Smith, Courtesy of the Amon Carter Museum).*

The dust of the drags, Three Block Range, near Richardson, New Mexico, 1908. Drag riding was dusty and unpleasant but essential to make sure none of the herd lagged behind *(by Erwin E. Smith, Courtesy of the Amon Carter Museum).*

herd and headed off the ranch. The cook boarded the chuck wagon and gave a slap of the reins.

The wagon rumbled down the road, kicking up a cloud of dust.

Nat and nine other cowboys moved to their spots as drag riders at the back of the herd. It was the worst position on the drive because it meant a whole day of riding through trail dust kicked up by three thousand generally uncooperative cattle. Tomorrow, however, he'd ride point at the front, the best spot. On the long trail ride to Dakota, he'd spend plenty of time in both positions.

"Hey," cowboys at the front yelled at the cattle. The animals didn't like mounted cowboys or their waving hats. They jumped to their feet.

Point riders took position at the front, on each side of the herd, and slowly moved toward each other, squeezing the front of the herd down to just six steer wide. The cattle wanted to spread out, but swing riders behind point riders moved in from either side, keeping the herd only a few animals wide and moving north.

Dawn was just breaking over the San Francisco mountains. Small triangles of sunlight shone on the plains, but most of the valley was still gray-green in darkness.

"Hey!" Cowboys yelled, waving their hats. Nat and the other drag riders kept their place, making sure none of the cattle decided they'd rather go south than north. It would be an hour or more before all the cattle were up and moving in the right direction. This drive would spread more than a mile along the trail.

Nat rested in his saddle, the reins hanging loosely. It didn't matter that he'd be riding drag his first day out. This was heaven.

Eleven

The night was pitch black except for the sudden jolts of light that flashed across the sky. Nat hunched over in the saddle, his fingers clutching the edges of his slicker against his neck. His Stetson, firmly planted on his head, offered little protection from the hail pelting his body. Some of the icy chunks slid down his shirt. The broad brim of the hat funneled pouring rain away from his face and maybe kept him a little drier, but he wasn't sure.

"What are the chances we don't have another stampede?" his buddy called to him.

"None," Nat said in disgust. This was the third thunderstorm in three nights, and the storms usually drove the cattle into a frenzy. Getting across Colorado wasn't easy in spring.

"I don't think I could chase those steer one more night," his buddy said. "I'd settle for a night of no sleep if I didn't have to get hammered by hail and chase those cattle."

Steer started pawing the earth. Nat felt the ground shake. "Easy, easy," he heard other cowboys trying to settle the cattle.

A low rumbling shook the earth. "All hands and cook!" the boss yelled.

It was a stampede.

Nat raced to the head of the herd. As one of the best and most experienced cowboys, he knew he'd be most able to head off the ornery cattle.

It seemed like forever that Nat and the other cowboys tried to turn the running cattle back into themselves to slow the stampede. Nat watched carefully to make sure he didn't get caught in the middle of the herd as it turned. A steer could trip his horse in an instant, and Nat would be thrown and trampled to death.

As quickly as the storm blew in, it blew by. The rampaging cattle slowed to a trot. Cowboys at the front of the herd got them to start circling toward the back. Cattle settled quickly when they milled, as the cowboys called it. The cowboys, bone tired after three sleepless nights, their clothes soaked by three nights of rain, formed a ring around the herd, and started singing softly to the cattle.

Stars twinkled in the sky. Nat looked for the North Star and saw the Big Dipper was low to the west. It was 2 AM. Nat moved away from the herd, now calmly resting in the field. Three hours of sleep sounded mighty good to him. He flopped on the ground, covered his head with his hat, and fell into a deep sleep.

*   *   *

For a month as they rode north, the Gallinger outfit heard that Lieutenant Colonel George Custer was somewhere ahead of them on the trail, headed to a showdown with Northern Cheyenne and Sioux Indians of the Great Plains. The U.S. military was under orders to move the Indians onto reservations. Sitting Bull, the great Hunkpapa Sioux warrior, had refused to settle on reservations created by the U.S. government and continued to lead resistance against white settlers moving into Dakota Territory.

Lieutenant Colonel George Custer, 1865 *(Courtesy of the Library of Congress).*

On June 25, as the Gallinger cowboys were sitting around their fire at day's end, they saw a man ride across the plains toward them. As he neared, they realized he was a government scout.

"Don't go any farther north," he advised the group. "Custer and the Indians are in a bloody battle. We can't be sure you won't get caught in the middle of it if you head that way."

The Arizona outfit headed to Dakota Territory. They arrived in the town of Deadwood, in the Black Hills, on July 3, 1876. There Nat learned Custer had been killed in the battle against Sitting Bull's warriors at Little Big Horn River in Montana. The cowboys had been about sixty miles away when the Seventh U.S. Cavalry, under Lieutenant Colonel Custer's command, had been defeated.

Once in Deadwood, the boss turned over three thousand head to the cattle's new owner, and cowboys lined up in front of the boss for their pay. With money in their pockets and a place to spend it, the next day, Independence Day, promised to be full of cowboy fun.

Nat rode into town with others, looking for the general store. He needed a new bandanna, he wanted new spurs, and he certainly was planning on a meal that didn't include beans, biscuits, or bacon.

"Hey, Red River Dick." Nat heard a familiar voice calling him from across the dusty main street. It was the trail boss. Nat walked over to talk to his buddy. "We have a little competition going outside of town," the boss said. "Some fellows chipped in and got a two-hundred-dollar pot. They want to see a little rodeo. Think you're up for it?"

Sitting Bull or *Ta-ton-ka-I-yo-tan-ka,* 1860–1880 *(Courtesy of the Library of Congress).*

"I just had three months of real, live rodeo all the way up from Arizona," Nat laughed.

After a long period of work on the range, the general merchandise store of the Greene Cattle Company, Hereford, Arizona, is a welcome sight to the cowboys, 1909 *(by Erwin E. Smith, Courtesy of the Amon Carter Museum).*

"Red, you know you're one of the best. Why don't you make your outfit proud?" his boss asked.

Nat grinned, "You know there's nothing I'd like better. I guess it'd be good fun on this Independence Day."

Cowboys from his outfit stood nearby. "Yeah, Red, you'll win for sure."

"Maybe so. Maybe I should back out and give some other cowboys a chance," Nat said, winking. "What kind of rodeo are we talking about anyway?"

"We'll have twelve cowboys and twelve mustangs in a corral. First cowboy to rope, throw, tie, saddle, bridle, and mount his mustang gets the pot," his boss said.

Nat looked around at all the weatherworn faces, eager for a good time. "Sounds great," he said. "Count me in."

$\mathcal{T}welve$

Nat picked out the best horse in their remuda, saddled it, and rode back to town. As he rode, he worked his lariat between his fingers, making sure no weak spots had developed along the thirty-foot leather rope. No point losing just because his lariat broke.

As Nat arrived, he saw a dozen mustangs pacing around the corral. "No easy horses in that bunch," Nat said, coming up to the fence. Cowboys from every different outfit hung on the fence, talking with one another. Miners in town for the holiday, their long beards ruffling in the wind, stood at one end of the enclosure, eager to see action. Three cowboys took turns lassoing a nearby tree stump, hoping it might give them an edge. Nat rode over to the boys from his outfit.

"You'll do great, Red," one of his fellow cowboys told him. "You've got gravel in your gizzard."

"This'll be like another day on the trail, that's all," said another. "We got you a saddle and bridle right here. We'll throw it up on the fence as soon as you get that critter roped."

"All right, boys," one of the trail bosses yelled. "Listen up. Cowboys competing for the prize—line up over here by the gate." Nat moved his horse into line, noting that six of the other competitors were also black cowboys, like him.

"As you fellows go into the corral, we'll point out the mustang you must rope, saddle, bridle, mount, and ride. A gun will fire one shot to give you the go. Fastest to mount wins the whole pot. There are no runners-up in this contest. You clear on the rules?"

The twelve cowboys nodded. Nat watched carefully to see which cowboy drew which mustang. First one and then the next drew what Nat thought was a fairly easy horse. Nat entered the ring astride his cutting horse. "Red River Dick, you get that bayo right there," the boss said.

"Holy smokes!" Nat said. "You didn't give me any break. No matter. I'll just ride like I'm on the range." The cowboys from his outfit laughed as Nat trotted to the other side of the corral.

Nat loosely knotted the reins over his saddle horn, held the loop of his lariat in one hand and the length of rope in the other.

All eyes were on the boss, who held his Colt aloft. "Ready! Set!"

Bang!

Nat spurred his horse forward and swung his

lariat. In the mad rush of horses, cowboys, and mustangs, Nat missed his first throw. His horse knew he missed and came to a dead stop while Nat recoiled his rope.

It cost him about a minute. Nat spurred his horse on and swung his lariat high.

Whoosh! It landed neatly over the bayo's head. Nat slipped the end over his saddle horn and dismounted. The mustang started to buck. Nat's horse dug his hooves into the dirt, almost sitting back on his

According to his autobiography, Nat Love was a remarkable marksman. He went on to win two shooting contests in Deadwood that day. This photograph was probably taken immediately after *(Courtesy of the Library of Congress)*.

hindquarters, to hold steady. Nat raced to the fence to grab the bridle and saddle and ran back to his own horse. He put one hand on the rope that connected his horse to the wild mustang and ran along it.

Everything happened so quickly that Nat could barely think, much less look around to see how other cowboys were doing. Now the hard part—sliding that bit into the bayo's mouth and strapping on the saddle.

Nat hadn't ridden a bucking bronco in years. It was a job reserved for young, green cowboys. But Nat had never forgotten the lessons he learned while just a teenager back in Tennessee. He jumped onto the mustang's back.

"We have a winner!" Nat heard the boss shout out. *Drat!* Nat thought, spurring the mustang, trying to settle it down. *I've let down my outfit.*

"Yeah, Red! You get 'em cowboy!" Nat looked around and realized he was the only one astride a mustang. The other eleven competitors were still trying to rope or saddle their broncos.

Nat whipped his hat off his head and started waving it in the air as the bronco kicked up its hooves. Cheers rose from the corral. "Yeehaw!" Nat yelled to the crowd.

"It took you nine minutes flat," the boss said. "That's mighty fast. I'd say you were the best cowboy around."

"Hey, hey!" All the cowboys cheered now. One yelled out, "That's Deadwood Dick! Best cowboy here in Dakota Territory, best in the West!"

Nat's grin was as wide as the open plains.

Postscript

On that centennial day, July 4, 1876, Nat, at twenty-two years of age, had broken the record for roping. In 1907 when he published his autobiography, *The Life and Adventures of Nat Love*, he claimed that no one had since beaten his time. He went on to win two shooting contests—one with his rifle and one with his revolver. According to Nat's autobiography, he hit fourteen of fourteen shots in the bull's eye with his rifle, which he claimed he held at his hip, a particularly difficult way to aim. When target shooting with his Colt 45, he placed ten of twelve shots in the bull's eye.

The life on the trail that Nat Love and other cowboys came to know right after the Civil War was short-lived, however. Two events dramatically changed cattle ranching in the West. The increased production of barbed wire in the 1880s and the expanding network of railroads across the West made cattle drives impossible and unnecessary. No longer could cowboys simply head out with cattle. Barbed wire roped off acres and acres of land, making cross-country travel impossible. And after the Civil War, railroads expanded their networks throughout the West. It was cheaper and easier to drive cattle a short distance to small railroad stations that had been built in Texas, Oklahoma, Colorado, and elsewhere, and ship cattle to one of the great meat-processing cities than to drive them hundreds of miles over the prairies to Dodge City, Kansas, or Abilene, Kansas, where the only rail stations had been. Cattle drives cost ranchers money: first, to pay for cowboys who drove the herds, and second, because the trail drives were hard on cattle, which often lost weight as they moved across country on the drive. "With the march of progress came the railroads," Nat wrote in his autobiography, "and no longer were we called upon to follow the long horned steers."

While Nat Love and other African Americans were important in exploring and settling the American West, they suffered the indignities of

Nat Love at the close of his railroad career *(Courtesy of Duke University).*

discrimination, nonetheless. Blacks, who made up the segregated U.S. Ninth and Tenth Cavalries and four infantry units created after the Civil War, later reorganized into the Twenty-fourth and Twenty-fifth Infantry, were known as Buffalo Soldiers. Their daily life was similar to white soldiers stationed on the plains, but their duties were often harder. Buffalo soldiers strung telegraph lines, built frontier outposts, and guarded crews building rail lines across the West. They made up twenty percent of the cavalry at that time. Even so, if a dispute arose between a buffalo soldier and a local white settler or lawman, the soldier invariably lost.

In 1890, Nat married and quit the cowboy life. He was thirty-four years old—quite old by cowboy standards. Few cowboys were older than thirty. Nat Love joined the industry that displaced cowboys— the railroads—and became a porter, at first on the

The Twenty-fourth Infantry at Fort Reno, Oklahoma Territory, 1890 *(Courtesy of the Fort Sill National Historic Landmark).*

Nat Love and his family *(Courtesy of Duke University).*

Denver and Rio Grande Railroad. He started working for the railroad for fifteen dollars a month—less than he was paid as a green cowboy some twenty years before. But this way Nat got to travel all over America. Nat also points out in his autobiography that on some rail trips later in his career, he made as much as seventy-five to one hundred and fifty dollars in tips.

Nat Love enjoyed every mile he traveled, first as a cowboy and then as a railroad porter. He was, through it all, a vocal and enthusiastic patriot. "It has always seemed strange to me that so many

Americans rush off to Europe and foreign countries each year in search of health and pleasure," he wrote in his book. "I always say to the traveling American, 'See America . . . Visit the capitol and let your chest swell with pride that you are an American . . .' I have seen a large part of America, and am still seeing it, but the life of a hundred years would be too short to see our country. America, I love thee, sweet land of liberty, home of the brave and the free."

Nat Love (far left) with an old cowboy friend and other friends at the close of his railroad career *(Courtesy of Duke University).*

Selected Bibliography

Blevins, Winfred. *Dictionary of the American West*. New York: Facts on File, 1993.

Forbis, William H. *The Cowboys*. Alexandria, VA: Time-Life Books, 1973.

Freedman, Russell. *Cowboys of the Wild West*. New York: Clarion Books, 1985.

Hook, Jason. *Sitting Bull and the Plains Indians*. New York: Bookwright Press, 1987.

Katz, William Loren. *The Black West*. New York: Touchstone, 1996.

Klausmeier, Robert. *Cowboy*. Minneapolis, MN: Lerner Publications, 1996.

Love, Nat. *The Life and Adventures of Nat Love, Better Known in the Cattle Country as Deadwood Dick*. Lincoln, NE: University of Nebraska Press, 1995.

Marin, Albert. *Cowboys, Indians and Gunfighters: The Story of the Cattle Kingdom*. New York: Atheneum, 1993.

Miller, Robert H. *Reflections of a Black Cowboy, Book One, Cowboys*. Silver Burdett Press: Englewood Cliffs, NJ: 1991.

Ravage, John W. *Black Pioneers*. Salt Lake City, UT: University of Utah Press, 1997.